AFRO-AMERICAN BOOK SOURCE
Your Black Bookstore By Mail
P.O. Box 851-S, Boston, MA 02120
(617) 442-3545

FAMOUS BLACK QUOTATIONS

and some not so famous

Famous Black Quotations

and some not so famous

selected and compiled
by
JANET CHEATHAM BELL

SABAYT PUBLICATIONS
1986

Grateful acknowledgement is made to those who granted permission to reprint excerpts from published works; and to people of African descent throughout the world and through the ages who continue to find strength in the Word.

© Copyright 1986 by Janet Cheatham Bell
All rights reserved

Printed and bound in the United States of America

First edition 9 8 7 6 5 4 3 2 1

ISBN: 0-9616649-9-1

Sabayt Publications
5441 S. Kenwood Avenue
Chicago, Illinois 60615

TO KAMAU
who is always searching for knowledge

Be skilled in speech so that you will succeed. The tongue of a man is his sword and effective speech is stronger than all fighting.

THE HUSIA

sacred wisdom of ancient Egypt

translated by Maulana Ron Karenga

CONTENTS

PREFACE ix

STRUGGLE 1

IDENTITY 21

SELF-RELIANCE 41

INDEX BY SUBJECT 63

INDEX BY NAME 66

Order Form 73

PREFACE

When did you last want a quotation by DuBois, Booker T., or Douglass, but didn't know where to find one?

How long has it been since you wanted to use a particular quotation in a lively conversation, but couldn't recall the exact words, or remember who said it?

Have you ever been writing a presentation at home, in the office, or on a plane and wanted to conclude with a quotation, but couldn't think of the right one?

If you have ever been in any of these predicaments, this is the book for you. Of the many and varied quotations by persons of African descent, over one hundred of the best known, including several that will become better known, have been collected here for your benefit and enjoyment.

This collection of quotations was begun after many unsuccessful attempts to locate specific quotations by African-Americans that I wanted for one project or another. Since standard reference works either did not include any quotations by people of African descent, or included only a small fraction of what was available, I saved what I had found for future use. As my collection grew, I began to respond to specific requests from family and friends. The natural next step was to publish them so that they could be shared with others who might be similarly frustrated.

Verifying the quotations for publication has been a labor of love because it has required not only that I read the works of many masters of language, but also that I listen attentively when black people gathered to listen to a speech or to converse.

Both reading and listening reinforced what I had always known, that multifarious images abound in the languages we use. These images are both fecund and powerful whether the quotation is from the oral tradition of an indigenous African language, or written/spoken in one of the several European languages that people of African descent have made their own.

Moreover, the matters that concern us have remained consistent over the centuries from ancient Egypt to the present, though the inaccessibility of these words of wisdom has limited our familiarity with their earlier forms.

This collection is compact to maximize its handiness, but there are many, many more where these came from. It is hoped that this small book represents a beginning of the collection and publication of quotations by people of African descent, and another indication of our respect for the potency of language.

I am grateful to Earle Pitts for the design, to Ursula McPike for the index, and to Laurie Wright for bringing me quotations. My family and my friends always believed that I would do it, but I received special encouragement from my mom, Anna Cheatham, and from Mildred Morgan Ball, Julian Bond, John H. Evans, Alvin and Lydia Foster, Deborah and Charles Stith, Madeline Scales Taylor, and my business partner and catalyst, Vinita Moch Ricks.

JCB

FAMOUS BLACK QUOTATIONS

STRUGGLE

> If there is no struggle, there is no progress.
>
> **FREDERICK DOUGLASS**

STRUGGLE

There are few things in the world as dangerous as sleepwalkers.

RALPH ELLISON

When you don't know when you have been spit on, it does not matter too much what else you think you know.

RUTH SHAYS

To name something is to wait for it in the place you think it will pass.

AMIRI BARAKA

The problem of the twentieth century is the problem of the color line.

W.E.B. DU BOIS

As long as an educated and wealthy Nigerian can be "Jim Crowed" in Johannesburg on his own ancestral continent or can still see a Ku Klux Klan cross burning in Mississippi, or until Africans have their proportionate share of posts on the great corporations that control their economies, or until one sees black faces among the top elites throughout the Arab world and in Hispanic America and Brazil where they are more rare now than in the racist United States, mobilization *as blacks* is still necessary. . . . Worldwide black consciousness is a psychological reserve that can be mobilized to achieve local ends as well as to aid others as the liberation process continues on.

ST. CLAIR DRAKE

4 STRUGGLE

I have a dream that my four little children will one day live in a nation where they will not be judged by the color of their skin, but by the content of their character.

MARTIN LUTHER KING, JR.

A community is democratic only when the humblest and weakest person can enjoy the highest civil, economic, and social rights that the biggest and most powerful possess.

A. PHILIP RANDOLPH

In our particular society, it is the narrowed and narrowing view of life that often wins.

ALICE WALKER

When unacquainted with other modes of life than their own meet with the record of such actions, unless they are restrained by authority, they look upon them as sins, and do not consider that their own customs either in regard to marriage, or feasts, or dress, or the other necessities and adornments of human life, appear sinful to the people of other nations and other times.

SAINT AUGUSTINE

Would America have been America without her Negro people?

W.E.B. DU BOIS

There are no good times to be black in America, but some times are worse than others.

DAVID BRADLEY

As legal slavery passed, we entered into a permanent period of unemployment and under employment from which we have yet to emerge.

JULIAN BOND

There is a debt to the Negro people which America can never repay. At least then, they must make amends.

SOJOURNER TRUTH

I have great fear for the moral will of Americans if it takes more than a week to achieve the results.

MICHAEL S. HARPER

The cost of liberty is less than the price of repression.

W.E.B. DU BOIS

Divestment is the one strategy that could bring about change with a minimum of violence. . . . The Sullivan Principles have made our chains more comfortable. What we want are the chains removed.

BISHOP DESMOND TUTU

While I am in favor of universal suffrage, yet I know that the colored man needs something more than a vote in his hand. . . . A man landless, ignorant and poor may use the vote against his interests; but with intelligence and land he holds in his hand the basis of power and elements of strength.

FRANCES ELLEN WATKINS HARPER

I cannot accept the definition of collective good as articulated by a privileged minority in society, especially when that minority is in power.

WOLE SOYINKA

It is an historical fact that whenever the oppressor is called upon to define an indigenous product of the oppressed that product loses its functional value.

JAMES G. SPADY

It grew on me that we, black men especially, were expected to be subservient even in groups where ostensibly everyone was equal.

SHIRLEY CHISHOLM

We wear the mask that grins and lies.

PAUL LAURENCE DUNBAR

No person is your friend who demands your silence, or denies your right to grow.

ALICE WALKER

Injustice anywhere is a threat to justice everywhere.

MARTIN LUTHER KING, JR.

What happens to a dream deferred?
Does it dry up
like a raisin in the sun?

LANGSTON HUGHES

I'm sick and tired of being sick and tired.

FANNIE LOU HAMER

The determination to outwit one's situation means that one has no models, only object lessons.

JAMES BALDWIN

The Negro pays for what he wants and begs for what he needs.

KELLY MILLER

Men may not get all they pay for in this world, but they must certainly pay for all they get.

FREDERICK DOUGLASS

If you want to keep something secret from black folks, put it between the covers of a book.

AFRICAN-AMERICAN FOLK SAYING

The Free in freedom
was put there
to blow your mind
to blow your game

MARI EVANS

A man who will not labor to
gain his rights, is a man who would
not, if he had them, prize and
defend them.

FREDERICK DOUGLASS

Has any Negro ever confessed that
civil rights can be a boring issue?
Necessary, yes, but boring as well
because it is war, and only the sick
can like war.

JOHN A. WILLIAMS

If there is no struggle, there is no progress. Those who profess to favor freedom, and yet deprecate agitation, are men who want crops without plowing up the ground. They want rain without thunder and lightning. They want the ocean without the awful roar of its many waters. This struggle may be a moral one; or it may be a physical one; or it may be both moral and physical; but it must be a struggle. Power concedes nothing without a demand.

FREDERICK DOUGLASS

Passion is not friendly. It is arrogant, superbly contemptuous of all that is not itself, and, as the very definition of passion implies the impulse to freedom, it has a mighty intimidating power. It contains a challenge. It contains an unspeakable hope.

JAMES BALDWIN

Fervor is the weapon of choice of the impotent.

FRANTZ FANON

Do not hurl a lance if you cannot aim correctly.

THE HUSIA

Strategy is better than strength.

HAUSA LEGEND

Our people have made the mistake of confusing the methods with the objectives. As long as we agree on objectives, we should never fall out with each other just because we believe in different methods or tactics or strategy. . . . We have to keep in mind at all times that we are not fighting for integration, nor are we fighting for separation. We are fighting for recognition as free humans in this society.

MALCOLM X

Negro action can be decisive. I say that we ourselves have the power to end the terror and to win for ourselves peace and security throughout the land.

PAUL ROBESON

Our nettlesome task is to discover how to organize our strength into compelling power.

MARTIN LUTHER KING, JR.

The doctrine that submission to violence is the best cure for violence did not hold good as between slaves and overseers. He was whipped oftener who was whipped easiest.

FREDERICK DOUGLASS

Men who are in earnest are not afraid of consequences.

MARCUS GARVEY

A man who won't die for something is not fit to live.

MARTIN LUTHER KING, JR.

I started with this idea in my head, "There's two things I've got a right to, death or liberty."

HARRIET TUBMAN

You had better all die — die immediately, than live slaves, and entail your wretchedness upon your posterity.

HENRY HIGHLAND GARNET

If we must die—let it not be
  like hogs
Hunted and penned in an inglorious
  spot

CLAUDE MC KAY

When elephants fight it is the grass
that suffers.

KIKUYU PROVERB

Real tragedy is never resolved. It
goes on hopelessly forever.

CHINUA ACHEBE

... What you seen
Wasn't no dust of changes rising.
It was the dust of sameness settling.

STERLING PLUMPP

Habit is heaven's own redress:
it takes the place of happiness.

ALEXANDER PUSHKIN

You cannot crack a pebble,
it excludes death . . . It will slay
 giants
but never bear children.

EDWARD KAMAU BRAITHWAITE

Voyage through death
            to life upon these shores.

ROBERT HAYDEN

While there's life, there's hope.

TERENCE *(Publius Terentius Afer)*

IDENTITY

Moulded on Africa's anvil,
tempered down home.

JULIAN BOND

IDENTITY

Africa my Africa . . .
I have never known you
But my face is full of your blood

DAVID DIOP

We are almost a nation of dancers, musicians, and poets.

OLAUDAH EQUIANO

These people have really a great deal of musical talent. Their songs and hymns are so wild, so strange, and yet so invariably harmonious and sweet. I never listen to "Roll Jordan Roll" without seeming to hear, almost to feel, the rolling of waters.

CHARLOTTE FORTEN GRIMKÉ

I, young in life, by seeming cruel fate
Was snatch'd from Afric's fancy'd happy seat.

PHILLIS WHEATLEY

The African, because of the violent differences between what was native and what he was forced to in slavery, developed some of the most complex and complicated ideas about the world imaginable.

AMIRI BARAKA

I must see [Africa], get close to it, because I can never lose the sense of being a displaced person here in America because of my color.

PAULE MARSHALL

IDENTITY

One feels his two-ness — an American, a Negro; two souls, two thoughts, two unreconciled strivings; two warring ideals in one dark body, whose dogged strength alone keeps it from being torn asunder.

W.E.B. DU BOIS

I who have cursed
The drunken officer of British rule,
  how choose
Between this Africa and the English
  tongue I love?

DEREK WALCOTT

And I . . . keep
wandering in the mystic rhythm
of jungle drums and the concerto.

GABRIEL OKARA

No two people on earth are alike,
and it's got to be that way in music
or it isn't music.

BILLIE HOLIDAY

Yet do I marvel at this curious
　thing:
To make a poet black, and bid him
　sing!

COUNTEE CULLEN

Had she paints, or clay, or knew the discipline of dance, or strings; had she anything to engage her tremendous curiosity and her gift for metaphor, she might have exchanged the restlessness and preoccupation with whim for any activity that provided her with all she yearned for. And like any artist with no art form, she became dangerous.

TONI MORRISON

Everytime I had the good fortune to research into someone's religion I found "God" to be the image of the people to whom the religion belongs; that is providing its philosophical concepts are indigenous, not colonial.

YOSEF BEN-JOCHANNON

They saw themselves as others had seen them. They had been formed by the images made of them by those who had had the deepest necessity to despise them.

JAMES BALDWIN

I am invisible, understand, simply because people refuse to see me.

RALPH ELLISON

I felt somehow for many years that George Washington and Alexander Hamilton just left me out by mistake. But through the process of amendment, interpretation and court decision, I have finally been included in "We, the people."

BARBARA JORDAN

Dependence had become a part of their second nature, and independence brought with it the cares and vexations of poverty.

ELIZABETH KECKLEY

A climate of alienation has a profound effect on the Black personality, particularly on the educated Black, who has the opportunity to see how the rest of the world regards him and his people. It often happens that the Black intellectual thus loses confidence in his own potential and that of his race. Often the effect is so crushing that some Blacks, having evidence to the contrary, still find it hard to accept the fact we really were the first to civilize the world.

CHEIKH ANTA DIOP

For some perverse reason, we children hated those marigolds. . . . Perhaps we had some dim notion of what we were, and how little chance we had of being anything else. Otherwise, why would we have been so preoccupied with destruction?

EUGENIA COLLIER

It is a very grave matter to be forced to imitate a people for whom you know — which is the price of your performance and survival — you do not exist. It is hard to imitate a people whose existence appears, mainly, to be made tolerable by their bottomless gratitude that they are not, thank heaven, *you*.

JAMES BALDWIN

History is a clock that people use to tell their time of day. It is a compass they use to find themselves on the map of human geography. It tells them where they are, and what they are.

JOHN HENRIK CLARKE

Intellectuals ought to study the past not for the pleasure they find in so doing, but to derive lessons from it.

CHEIKH ANTA DIOP

The black man who wants to turn his race white is as miserable as he who preaches hatred for the whites.

FRANTZ FANON

IDENTITY

A child born under oppression has all the elements of servility in its constitution.

MARTIN DELANY

If you have no confidence in self you are twice defeated in the race of life. With confidence you have won even before you have started.

MARCUS GARVEY

Your world is as big as you make it.

GEORGIA DOUGLAS JOHNSON

Those whom the gods would destroy they first call "promising."

JAN CAREW

When you control a man's thinking you do not have to worry about his actions. You do not have to tell him not to stand here or go yonder. He will find his "proper place" and will stay in it. You do not need to send him to the back door. He will go without being told. In fact, if there is no back door, he will cut one for his special benefit.

CARTER G. WOODSON

He who fears is literally delivered to destruction.

HOWARD THURMAN

I have
never been contained
except I
made
the prison

MARI EVANS

Don't look back. Something may be
gaining on you.

SATCHEL PAIGE

It is impossible to pretend that you
are not heir to, and therefore,
however inadequately or unwillingly,
responsible to, and for, the time
and place that give you life—
without becoming, at very best, a
dangerously disoriented human
being.

JAMES BALDWIN

How I wish I could pigeon-hole myself
and neatly fix a label on!
But self-knowledge comes too late
and by the time I've known myself
I am no longer what I was.

MABEL SEGUN

When I discover who I am, I'll be free.

RALPH ELLISON

I would never be of any service to anyone as a slave.

NAT TURNER

Too many black folks are fools about color and hair.

MABEL LINCOLN

I am a man who perceives life in a certain way, a man who rejects things that defecate on humankind, who rejects anything that will not give people room for dissent.

HARRY BELAFONTE

I must oppose any attempt that Negroes may make to do to others what has been done to them. . . . I know the spiritual wasteland to which that road leads . . . *whoever debases others is debasing himself.*

JAMES BALDWIN

The pasts of his ancestors lean against
Him. Crowd him. Fog out his identity.

GWENDOLYN BROOKS

From adolescence to death there is something very personal about being a Negro in America.

> **J. SAUNDERS REDDING**

I am not a perfect servant. I am a public servant.

> **JESSE JACKSON**

The basic tenet of black consciousness is that the black man must reject all value systems that seek to make him a foreigner in the country of his birth and reduce his basic human dignity.

> **STEVE BIKO**

Color is not a human or a personal reality; it is a political reality.

JAMES BALDWIN

In America, black *is* a country.

AMIRI BARAKA

I am not tragically colored. There is no great sorrow dammed up in my soul, nor lurking behind my eyes. I do not mind at all. . . . I do not weep at the world—I am too busy sharpening my oyster knife.

ZORA NEALE HURSTON

Our people know that they are the worthy repositories of human culture, assets in the defense and perpetuity of which so large a number of our ancestors—forever immortal—gave their lives; our people did not kneel to the cultural mystification of the authorities in occupation.

SÉKOU TOURÉ

Say it loud. I'm black and I'm proud.

JAMES BROWN

I believe in pride of race and lineage and self: in pride of self so deep as to scorn injustice to other selves. Especially do I believe in the Negro Race: in the beauty of its genius, the sweetness of its soul, and its strength in that meekness which shall yet inherit this turbulent earth.

W.E.B. DU BOIS

SELF-RELIANCE

It is far better to be free to govern, or misgovern, yourself than to be governed by anybody else.

KWAME NKRUMAH

A child who is to be successful is not reared exclusively on a bed of down.

AKAN PROVERB

No greater injury can be done to any youth than to let him feel that because he belongs to this or that race he will be advanced in life regardless of his own merits or efforts.

BOOKER T. WASHINGTON

One's work may be finished some day, but one's education never.

ALEXANDRE DUMAS, *pere*

For colored people to acquire learning in this country makes tyrants quake and tremble on their sandy foundation.

DAVID WALKER

The impulse to dream had been slowly beaten out of me by experience. Now it surged up again and I hungered for books, new ways of looking and seeing.

RICHARD WRIGHT

Education is our passport to the future, for tomorrow belongs to the people who prepare for it today.

MALCOLM X

The so called modern education, with all its defects, however, does others so much more good than it does the Negro because it has been worked out in conformity to the needs of those who have enslaved and oppressed weaker peoples.

CARTER G. WOODSON

Racial and denominational schools impart to the membership of their communities something which the general educational institution is wholly unable to inculcate.

KELLY MILLER

It is the fool whose own tomatoes are sold to him.

AKAN PROVERB

At the bottom of education, at the bottom of politics, even at the bottom of religion, there must be for our race economic independence.

BOOKER T. WASHINGTON

We must not only be able to black boots, but to make them.

FREDERICK DOUGLASS

A man's bread and butter is only insured when he works for it.

MARCUS GARVEY

Treat your guest as a guest for two days; on the third day, give him a hoe!

SWAHILI FOLK SAYING

It's easy to work for somebody else; all you have to do is show up.

RITA WARFORD

Actually we are slaves to the cost of living.

CAROLINA MARIA DE JESUS

Man cannot live by profit alone.

JAMES BALDWIN

Cease to be a drudge, seek to be an artist.

MARY MCLEOD BETHUNE

Jazz] music has always been for me, as well as most black writers, an inspiration. . . . The ideas that emerge magically from this music often provide clarity in the work I am doing.

PAUL CARTER HARRISON

I don't sing a song unless I feel it. The song don't tug at my heart, I pass on it. I have to believe in what I'm doing.

RAY CHARLES

Business? It's quite simple. It's other people's money.

ALEXANDRE DUMAS, *fils*

The appearance of millionaires in any society is no proof of its affluence; they can be produced by very poor countries. . . . It is not efficiency of production which makes millionaires; it is the uneven distribution of what is produced.

JULIUS K. NYERERE

He who starts behind in the great race of life must forever remain behind or run faster than the man in front.

BENJAMIN E. MAYS

Land tenure is the key to the Gikuyu people's life; it secures for them that peaceful tillage of the soil which supplies their material needs and enables them to perform their magic and traditional ceremonies in undisturbed serenity, facing Mount Kenya.

JOMO KENYATTA *(Kamau Wa Ngengi)*

Every race and every nation should be judged by the best it has been able to produce, not by the worst.

JAMES WELDON JOHNSON

No race can prosper till it learns that there is as much dignity in tilling a field as in writing a poem.

BOOKER T. WASHINGTON

If a man is called to be a streetsweeper, he should sweep streets even as Michelangelo painted, or Beethoven composed music, or Shakespeare wrote poetry. He should sweep streets so well that all the hosts of heaven and earth will pause to say, here lived a great streetsweeper who did his job well.

MARTIN LUTHER KING, JR.

Mastery of language affords remarkable power.

FRANTZ FANON

Words spoken without meaning have no tentacles. They float endlessly, bouncing here and there, restless pieces of the spirit; sent out without any mission or specific destination, landing no where and serving no purpose, except to diminish the spirit of the speaker.

J.C. BELL

Thought is more important than art. . . . To revere art and have no understanding of the process that forces it into existence, is finally not even to understand what art is.

AMIRI BARAKA

Art for art's sake is just another piece of deodorised dog-shit.

CHINUA ACHEBE

Although the way of God is before all people, the fool cannot find it.

THE HUSIA

The specialism and visible success of the sciences have impressed some minds to such a degree that they have virtually identified the possibilities of human knowledge with the possibilities of science.

> W.E. ABRAHAM

Children see things very well sometimes—and idealists even better.

> LORRAINE HANSBERRY

Wisdom is not like money to be tied up and hidden.

> AKAN PROVERB

The friend of a fool is a fool. The friend of a wise person is another wise person.

THE HUSIA

A man must be at home somewhere before he can feel at home everywhere.

HOWARD THURMAN

Before a group can enter the open society, it must first close ranks.

STOKELY CARMICHAEL

CHARLES V. HAMILTON

In all things that are purely social we can be as separate as the fingers, yet one as the hand in all things essential to mutual progress.

BOOKER T. WASHINGTON

Chance has never yet satisfied the hope of a suffering people. Action, self-reliance, the vision of self and the future have been the only means by which the oppressed have seen and realized the light of their own freedom.

MARCUS GARVEY

The political philosophy of black nationalism means that the black man should control the politics and the politicians in his own community; no more.

MALCOLM X

We realize that our future lies chiefly in our own hands. We know that neither institution nor friends can make a race stand unless it has strength in its own foundation; that races like individuals must stand or fall by their own merit; that to fully succeed they must practice the virtues of self-reliance, self-respect, industry, perseverance, and economy.

PAUL ROBESON

Life is a short walk. There is so little time and so much living to achieve.

JOHN OLIVER KILLENS

I have only just a minute,
Only sixty seconds in it,
Forced upon me—can't refuse it,
Didn't seek it, didn't choose it.
But it's up to me to use it.
I must suffer if I lose it.
Give account if I abuse it,
Just a tiny little minute—
But eternity is in it.

BENJAMIN E. MAYS

Do not count your chickens before they are hatched.

AESOP

We must reinforce argument with results.

BOOKER T. WASHINGTON

Time is neutral and does not change things. With courage and initiative, leaders change things.

JESSE JACKSON

Who would be free themselves must strike the blow.

FREDERICK DOUGLASS

Power in defense of freedom is greater than power in behalf of tyranny and oppression.

MALCOLM X

You may write me down in history
With your bitter, twisted lies,
You may trod me in the very dirt
But still, like dust, I'll rise.

     MAYA ANGELOU

The very time I thought I was lost,
my dungeon shook and my chains
fell off.

AFRICAN-AMERICAN FOLK SAYING

Not that success, for him, is sure,
 infallible.
But never has he been afraid to reach.
His lesions are legion.
But reaching is his rule.

     GWENDOLYN BROOKS

If now isn't a good time for the truth I don't see when we'll get to it.

NIKKI GIOVANNI

Up, up, you mighty race! You can accomplish what you will.

MARCUS GARVEY

Nothing succeeds like success.

ALEXANDRE DUMAS, *pere*

If you cain't bear no crosses,
You cain't wear no crown.

AFRICAN-AMERICAN SPIRITUAL

Let a new earth rise. Let another world be born. Let a bloody peace be written in the sky. Let a second generation full of courage issue forth; let a people loving freedom come to growth.

MARGARET WALKER

INDEX

SUBJECT
Africa, 21, 22, 23, 24, 49
America, 5, 6, 7, 36, 37
art, 22, 25, 26, 47, 52

color, 2, 3, 4, 23, 25, 30, 34, 36, 37
commitment, 12, 17, 61
conflict, 18, 23, 24, 25, 34

deception, 9, 18, 19, 31, 45

economics, 45, 46, 48
education, 42, 43, 44
excellence, 47, 48, 49, 50

freedom, 3, 7, 12, 13, 14, 15, 17, 23, 28, 33, 34, 41, 55, 59
future, 4, 18, 19, 29, 33, 43, 56, 60

history, 5, 18, 21, 28, 30, 35, 38
hope, 4, 14, 19, 59

justice, 4, 6, 8, 10, 27

knowledge, 2, 11, 28, 30, 52, 53, 54

language, v, 2, 8, 9, 24, 51
life, 4, 5, 19, 35, 42, 48, 49, 57

music, 22, 25, 47, 61

INDEX

nationalism, 37, 41, 54, 56

oppression, 4, 6, 7, 9, 10, 27, 28, 29, 31, 32, 43, 44, 46, 58

perception, 4, 5, 26, 27, 29, 36, 49, 53, 60
power, 8, 13, 14, 16, 56, 57
pride, 9, 11, 30, 35, 37, 38, 39
progress, 1, 13, 27, 55, 58

resistance, 7, 10, 11, 12, 13, 15, 16, 18, 34, 35, 36, 58, 59
responsibility, 8, 11, 12, 16, 28, 33, 42, 45, 55, 56, 57, 58

strategy, 7, 8, 9, 11, 14, 15, 18, 19
success, v, 31, 32, 42, 56, 58, 59, 60

thought, 2, 24, 26, 32, 52

work, 6, 42, 45, 46, 50, 57

NAME
Abraham, W.E., 53
Achebe, Chinua, 18, 52
Aesop, 57
African-American, 11, 59, 61
Akan, 42, 45, 53
Angelou, Maya, 59
Augustine, Saint, 5

Baldwin, James, 11, 14, 27, 29, 33, 35, 37, 46
Baraka, Amiri, 2, 23, 37, 52
Belafonte, Harry, 35
Bell, J.C., 51
Bethune, Mary McLeod, 47
Biko, Steve, 36
Bond, Julian, 6, 21
Bradley, David, 6
Braithwaite, Edward Kamau, 19
Brooks, Gwendolyn, 35, 59
Brown, James, 38

Carew, Jan, 31
Carmichael, Stokely, 54
Charles, Ray, 47

Chisholm, Shirley, 9
Clarke, John Henrik, 30
Collier, Eugenia, 29
Cullen, Countee, 25

Delany, Martin, 31
Diop, Cheikh Anta, 28, 30
Diop, David, 22
Douglass, Frederick, 1, 11, 12, 13, 16, 45, 58
Drake, St. Clair, 3
DuBois, W.E.B., 2, 5, 7, 24, 39
Dumas, Alexandre, *fils,* 48
Dumas, Alexandre, *pere,* 42, 60
Dunbar, Paul Laurence, 9

Ellison, Ralph, 2, 27, 34
Equiano, Olaudah, 22
Evans, Mari, 12, 33

Fanon, Frantz, 14, 30, 51

Garnet, Henry Highland, 17
Garvey, Marcus, 17, 31, 45, 55, 60

Giovanni, Nikki, 60
Grimké, Charlotte Forten, 22

Hamer, Fannie Lou, 10
Hamilton, Charles V., 54
Hansberry, Lorraine, 53
Harper, Frances Ellen Watkins, 8
Harper, Michael S., 7
Harrison, Paul Carter, 47
Hausa, 15
Hayden, Robert, 19
Holiday, Billie, 25
Hughes, Langston, 10
Hurston, Zora Neale, 37
Husia, The, v, 14, 52, 54

Jackson, Jesse, 36, 58
Jesus, Carolina Maria de, 46
Jochannon, Yosef ben-, 26
Johnson, Georgia Douglas, 31
Johnson, James Weldon, 49
Jordan, Barbara, 27

Keckley, Elizabeth, 28

Kenyatta, Jomo, 49
Kikuyu, 18
Killens, John Oliver, 57
King, Martin Luther, Jr., 4, 10, 16, 17, 50

Lincoln, Mabel, 34

Marshall, Paule, 23
Mays, Benjamin E., 48, 57
McKay, Claude, 18
Miller, Kelly, 11, 44
Morrison, Toni, 26

Nkrumah, Kwame, 41
Nyerere, Julius K., 48

Okara, Gabriel, 25

Paige, Satchel, 33
Plumpp, Sterling, 18
Pushkin, Alexander, 19

Randolph, A. Philip, 4
Redding, J. Saunders, 36
Robeson, Paul, 16, 56

Segun, Mabel, 34
Shays, Ruth, 2
Soyinka, Wole, 8
Spady, James G., 9
Swahili, 46

Terence, 19
Thurman, Howard, 32, 54
Truth, Sojourner, 6
Touré, Sékou, 38
Tubman, Harriet, 17
Turner, Nat, 34
Tutu, Bishop Desmond, 7

Walcott, Derek, 24
Walker, Alice, 4, 10
Walker, David, 43
Walker, Margaret, 61
Warford, Rita, 46
Washington, Booker T., 42, 45, 50, 55, 58

Wheatley, Phillis, 23
Williams, John A., 12
Wright, Richard, 43
Woodson, Carter G., 32, 44

X, Malcolm, 15, 43, 56, 58

You may order single copies of **FAMOUS BLACK QUOTATIONS**, or a hundred copies or more for your church, sorority, fraternity, or community organization fundraiser.

☐ Please send me _____ copies of **FAMOUS BLACK QUOTATIONS** at **$5.25** each, plus **$1.25** each for shipping and handling.

☐ My organization would like _____ copies of **FAMOUS BLACK QUOTATIONS** at the discount rate of **$4.00** each (minimum order 100 copies; includes shipping and handling costs).

_____

your name   phone: area code/number

_____

shipping address   city   state   zip

_____

name of organization

Amount enclosed $ _____

Include payment with order. Please do not send cash. Make checks or money orders payable to SABAYT PUBLICATIONS. Mail to:

Sabayt Publications
5441 S. Kenwood Avenue
Chicago, Illinois 60615

(PLEASE ALLOW 6-8 WEEKS FOR DELIVERY.)

You may order single copies of FAMOUS BLACK QUOTATIONS, or a hundred copies or more for your church, sorority, fraternity, or community organization fundraiser.

☐ Please send me _____ copies of FAMOUS BLACK QUOTATIONS at $5.25 each, plus $1.25 each for shipping and handling.

☐ My organization would like _____ copies of FAMOUS BLACK QUOTATIONS at the discount rate of $4.00 each (minimum order 100 copies; includes shipping and handing costs).

your name			phone: area code/number
shipping address	city	state	zip
name of organization			
Amount enclosed $			

Include payment with order. Please do not send cash. Make checks or money orders payable to SABAYT PUBLICATIONS. Mail to:

Sabayt Publications
5441 S. Kenwood Avenue
Chicago, Illinois 60615

(PLEASE ALLOW 6-8 WEEKS FOR DELIVERY.)

"Sabayt" is a transliteration of several ancient Egyptian hieroglyphs that mean "instruction," "transferring wisdom," "understanding."

SABAYT PUBLICATIONS is dedicated to disseminating only those materials that contribute to the increased knowledge and understanding of the history, culture, and thought of people of African descent.

Janet Cheatham Bell's parents brought home hard-to-come-by books by African-American writers during her childhood, thus igniting for her a lifetime study of the history and culture of African-Americans.

She has taught African-American literature at a number of colleges and universities, and been associate editor of *The Black Scholar*. In 1972, with St. Clair Drake and Ronald W. Bailey at Stanford University, she authored the curriculum review, *Teaching Black*. Until 1984 she was a senior editor of literature textbooks with Ginn and Company, Boston.

Ms. Bell currently lives in Chicago where she is a freelance writer and editor.